collective

Contemporary Styles Series

CD INCLUDED

Contemporary Rock Styles For the Bass

by Gary Kelly

T0087890

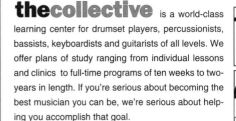

thecollective is a world-class learning center for drumset players, percussionists, bassists, keyboardists and guitarists of all levels. We offer plans of study ranging from individual lessons and clinics to full-time programs of ten weeks to two-years in length. If you're serious about becoming the best musician you can be, we're serious about helping you accomplish that goal.

**541 Avenue of the Americas,
New York, NY 10011
T: 212-741-0091**

www.thecoll.com

Executive Producer – *Lauren Keiser*
Executive Co-producer – *John Costellano*
Author Liason – *Tony Maggiolino*
Creative Director – *Alex Teploff*
Managing Editor – *Nicholas Hopkins*
Production Editor – *Seth Goldberg*
Cover Design – *Andrew J. Dowty*
Book Design – *Andrew J. Dowty*
Production Designer – *Andy Ray Wong*
Photo of New York City – *Maureen Plainfield*
Other Photography – *Andy Dowty and Kyung Chul-Choi*
Production Coordinator and Audio Engineer – *Tony Conniff*

CARL FISCHER®

65 Bleecker Street, New York, NY 10012

ISBN 0-8258-6268-X

TABLE OF CONTENTS

Foreword 3

Introduction 3

Author's Foreword 4

Introduction to the Musical Style of Rock 'n' Roll 4

Techniques and Equipment Setup..5

Bass Inspiration 6

How to Use This Book...7

About Gary Kelly 7

Sub-Style No. 1: Straight Eighth-Note Feel with Stop Time 8

Sub-Style No. 2: Medium Rock Stomp 10

Sub-Style No. 3: Rock Ballad 12

Sub-Style No. 4: Funk Rock 14

Sub-Style No. 5: Heavy Rock 16

Sub-Style No. 6: Traditional Shuffle 18

Sub-Style No. 7: Hard Rock Shuffle 20

Sub-Style No. 8: $\frac{12}{8}$ Slow Blues (Minor) 22

Sub-Style No. 9: 2-Beat 24

Sub-Style No. 10: Train Beat (Country Shuffle) 26

Sub-Style No. 11: "Bo Diddley" Beat..28

Sub-Style No. 12: New Orleans Second Line 30

Sub-Style No. 13: Up-tempo Rock-Swing with Stop Time (Rockabilly) 32

Sub-Style No. 14: Reggae 34

Sub-Style No. 15: Rockin' Odd Meters 36

Selected Discography 38

Selected Bibliography 38

Performers on the CD:

Gary Kelly – Bass
Sandy Gennaro – Drums
Kenny Brescia – Guitar

FOREWORD

The Collective was established in 1977 by a small group of professional New York musicians, who wanted to pool their energies and create a place where young drummers, and later bass, guitar, and keyboard students, could study and prepare themselves for a career in music. Since opening its doors, The Collective has graduated thousands of students, who have gone on to establish themselves in the world of professional music. I don't think that it is immodest to say that our alumni are helping to shape the direction that popular music is taking around the world.

Over the years the curriculum at The Collective has evolved to include a wide range of courses focusing on everything from technique and reading, to the study of all the important contemporary and ethnic styles. This book, along with our other Rhythm Section based books, covers the material offered in the Collective's Certificate Program.

The styles offered here represent the key styles in the contemporary idiom. Since all styles have tended to grow out of each other, and mutually influence each other, the student will find common threads that link them all together and make it easier to absorb and make them part of a young musician's personal style signature.

Each book contains a brief biography of the author, who is the faculty member who teaches this style at The Collective. You will also find a brief introduction to the general style and examples of the various substyles to be studied. Woven throughout the material are performance tips that come out of the teacher's years of experience. The most important element, however, are the pre-recorded rhythm-section CDs, on which our teachers perform with other musicians who also specialize in playing the style. Listening to and practicing with these CDs are the most important things for you to do to develop skills playing in the style. Music notation and the written word can, at best, only help you derive an intellectual understanding of the music. It is in listening to the actual music that you will come to understand it. In this regard, we strongly encourage you to make an effort to listen to the music listed in the recommended discography at the end of each section. The blank staves are meant for you to notate your own personal variations for each style. First, you must learn the pure style; then, you can adapt it to your own musical needs.

I would like to express my appreciation to all the teachers who have, over the years, contributed to the growth of the Collective and to this program in particular. I would also like to thank the hard working and talented folks at Carl Fischer for supporting our effort to get it right, and doing such a fine job with this book. Finally, I would like to thank Tony Maggiolino of our staff for all his hard work in coordinating all the material, and struggling to meet ever looming deadlines.

—John Castellano.
Director, The Collective

Author's Foreword

To become a proficient Rock bassist it is important to define what a Rock bassist is. The elusive nature of a single definition is due to the many influences that come together to form the style of music we know as Rock. Because of this it is important as a Rock bassist to be aware of the many styles Rock draws its influences from, and, more importantly, know what is the expected role of the bass in these styles. How does it relate to Rock as each of us knows and plays it? What are the rhythmic and harmonic clichés that define a style's contribution to Rock's family tree? For instance, you don't have to be a jazz bass player to play Rock. But it would certainly be very helpful to understand the concept of swing, especially how it is applied in Boogie Rock, Country Rock, Jazz Rock, and most importantly, Blues Rock. This applies to all the different styles and variations covered in this book. The idea is to give you, the musician, an understanding of how Rock bass lines are formed and provide you with a palette of useful ideas that you can rework and adapt to come up with your own original lines and style. Every Rock band, no matter how original, has influences that they have drawn from. Knowing the history of the style will allow you to go forward, creating a fresh take on a form that as it grows older, struggles to expand and continue to be relevant as a form of entertainment in our society.

—Gary Kelly

Introduction to the Musical Style of Rock 'n' Roll

Rock & Roll, or simply Rock for our purposes, is composed of recognizable patterns, rhythmic and harmonic clichés. These give Rock its signature sound that allows us to see it as a distinct style. Rock draws its influences from many different styles and periods of music. These contributions make up the different rhythmic, harmonic and technical building blocks. They can be shuffled, reorganized and reshaped as the musician sees fit. A typical Rock groove can be expanded and modified just by varying the rhythm that either the bass or drums are playing. If the drummer plays the same pattern for sixteen bars, the bass can play eight bars of, let's say, a quarter-note feel and eight bars of an eighth-note feel. This can provide the rhythmic diversity to distinguish between two different sections of the song, verse and chorus, chorus and bridge, verse and verse variation. The ability to interchange rhythms from different sources and recombine them with the drums allows for a myriad number of different sub-styles of the music we call Rock. A player's ability to understand the material available and be creative in coming up with new ways of arranging and presenting it are the core to being successful playing Rock music.

The "mutt" of musical styles, it's an amalgamation of ideas from different musical sources that comes together to be known as Rock. Through its history, Rock's roots can be traced back to early twentieth-century Blues and Jazz. Gospel, Rhythm & Blues and Country have also made generous contributions, hence the splintering of Rock into numerous sub-styles. Ask any two musicians to define Rock and you will get two different answers. Rock is many things to many people. This style is also known by its many aliases. Whether it is called Doo-wop, Boogie-Woogie, Boogaloo, Rockabilly, Pop Rock, Girl Groups, Surf Music, Folk Rock, Psychedelic Rock, Jazz Rock, Alternative, New Wave, Hardcore, Punk Rock, Hard Rock, Acid Rock, Metal, Speed Metal, Death Metal, Funk Rock, Blues Rock, Latin Rock, New Orleans Rock, Progressive Rock, Classic Rock, Country Rock, Southern Rock, English Rock, Glam Rock; the list could go on, and does continue to go on as new combinations of styles become popular. This book does not attempt to cover every sub-style of Rock. What it does do is present a cross section of different building blocks that have been part of the foundation of Rock. By mastering this material one will acquire a more diverse set of fundamental harmonic and rhythmic ideas with which to build more interesting Rock bass lines.

Techniques and Equipment Setup

Technique

Rock bass playing, like any other style, demands some basic knowledge of the instrument and how to get a sound out of it. This book assumes that an aspiring bassist will have already mastered or at least investigated the basics of harmony and theory in respect to how they shape playing the bass.

An aspiring bassist should:
- Know all the notes on the bass,
- Be able to play all the basic scales (Major, Dominant/Mixolydian, Lydian, Natural Minor/Aeolian, Dorian, Phrygian, Pentatonic, Blues), in any key, two octaves.
- Understand the 12-bar Blues form, and be able to play it in a variety of grooves.
- Be able to groove and keep time with a metronome in a variety of styles.

Equipment Setup

Personal taste has a lot to do with what tools we choose to express our musicality. The world of Rock has many classics as well as latest trends that are all valid. Rock has fueled the fortunes of many a music-equipment manufacturer, such as Fender, Marshall, Gibson, Ampeg, and Rickenbacker. Everyone has their favorite brands that they swear is the essence of Rock, for example a Fender bass and an Ampeg SVT or a Hofner with a Vox amp.

Combining the equipment with other aspects of sound, like: fretted or fretless, four, five or six string, electric, acoustic, plucked, picked, slapped, tapped, strummed, hammered, pure and natural in tone and every shade of banshee wail, warble, thump, boom and thud this side of the gates of hell — all this has a place somewhere in the sound-world of Rock. Also, there is the ever-present debate about action/string height. When does low and easy-to-play action become incapable of providing a fat bass tone? New strings are too bright, old strings are too dead, yet both have legions of devotees.

There are many paths to investigate when choosing the equipment that will be your sound. Many bassists are collectors, who own dozens, even hundreds, of instruments and scores of amps, each with their own unique characteristics. Other bassists are known for their devotion to one brand or even one particular instrument. Choosing the same equipment as your idols can yield good results for a beginner who is not sure what his style is yet. Ultimately your equipment and how you utilize it becomes a personal matter of what you need to express your vision of what the function of the bass in music is. There are many models to choose from whether we are wild soloists or backline groovers. Whatever makes you comfortable when you play is the answer for you.

Bass Inspiration

There are many great rock bassists, too many to begin to mention them all here. Some players are known for certain techniques or styles. Here are just a few sources of inspiration when you feel musically or technically stale.

Heavy Dudes

Geezer Butler, John Paul Jones, Felix Pappalardi, Gene Simmons

The Top Picks

Joe Osborn, Carol Kay, Anthony Jackson, Steve Swallow, Paul McCartney, Chris Squire, Geddy Lee, Phil Lesh, Lee Sklar, John Entwhistle

Finger-Style Stars

Jack Bruce, James Jamerson, Jaco Pastorius, Donald "Duck" Dunn, Franco Rocco Prestia, Berry Oakley

Thumpers and Slappers

Larry Graham, Flea, Stanley Clark, Les Claypool, Marcus Miller, Victor Wooten

Tappers

Billy Sheehan, Michael Manring, Stu Hamm

Fretless Wizards

Jaco Pastorius, Jack Bruce, Pino Palladino, Andy Frazier

Deep Groove

George Porter, Aston Barrett. Robbie Shakespeare, Chuck Rainey

Acoustic Masters

Charles Mingus, Ray Brown, Jimmy Blanton, Willie Dixon, Slam Stewart, Charlie Haden, Dave Holland

How To Use This Book

The styles in this book each have their own demo track and play-along track. The demo track has my bass part as notated on the chart. In most cases, for the demo form we play through each section of the song once without repeats. The play-along track has no bass. The form on the chart is accurate for the play-along track. You can play along reading the bass line provided. However, in many cases there is more than one repetition of sections. You would not want to keep playing the exact same bass line. The chord changes are provided for you to create your own lines. If you investigate the sources of these styles as well as doing the prep exercises and playing along with the tracks, you will acquire a wider vocabulary and have more choices available to you in creating new lines.

In the Prepatory Exercises I suggest using a metronome, although a drum machine would work as well. I think that when learning new grooves, it is important to have a rhythmic point of reference to keep us honest. The reference should allow you more freedom with the time. It is important to become comfortable with playing behind the beat and in front of the beat. It's what makes the groove come alive; the human element. Don't allow the metronome to make you play stiffly or mechanically. It is only a reference that allows us to check our time, listening to another sound at the same time as playing our part. The relaxed feel achieved by playing behind the beat is a major part of much of Rock. The tension and excitement built by playing on top of the beat is also a much used device in Rock. Knowing how to utilize the full range of the beat and mastering it is what makes your playing diverse. Dynamics are another essential device for building excitement and holding an audience's attention. Rock is made up of many facets. This book will provide you with a basic understanding of the style and a jumping-off point for deeper exploration of this style and musical exploration in general.

About Gary Kelly

Udo Geisler Fotografie

Gary plays four- and six-string fretted and fretless electric basses and acoustic bass. He studied basic music and acoustic bass at Pennsylvania State University and graduated from the Berklee College of Music in Boston with a B.A. in Performance/Composition.

He's performed with numerous Rock/Pop artists such as The Mama's & Papa's, Jimmy Buffet, The Platters, The Teenagers, The Crystals, and Martha Reeves and the Vandella's. On the Jazz scene he's worked with Bill Frisell, Tony Purrone, Mike Stern, The Tom Pierson Orchestra (featured on the Smithsonian Big Band Collection), The Ed Palermo Big Band, and Leroy Jenkins. Also active on the blues scene he's worked with Popa Chubby and as bassist and musical director/producer for Pat Tortorici. In the field of World Music Gary has played with Bobby Sanabria and Ascencion, José José, Nostos, Ana Baboula, Haydah and Daryush.

Gary is currently teaching and developing courses at The Collective in New York City. Along with Rock Bass, he also teaches bass private lessons, Beginner Bass, Studio Bass 1 & 2. Other classes include Bass Technique: Jazz, Rock, Blues & Funk, Studio Drumming 1 & 2, Drum / Bass private lessons, Digital Audio for Musicians; Studio Skills and Studio Rhythm Section. He's also the Recording Studio Manager/Chief Engineer at The Collective NYC.

SUB-STYLE NO. 1:
Straight Eighth-note Feel with Stop Time

Brief History

This style has its roots in Jazz, Jump Blues and Boogie Woogie-Swing. This style, through the work of some of its stars like Chuck Berry, Muddy Waters, Howlin' Wolf and Bo Diddley, established the guitar as the new voice of popular music. The bass at this point was a rhythmic instrument more felt than an audible one. However, the rhythmic underpinning and drive it provided became a vital part of what we call Rock.

Preparatory Exercises

Arpeggios are a big part of this style and should be practiced with the metronome to build speed, clarity and stamina. Besides the arpeggios there are many simple connecting phrases that are from the walking bass/jazz school. Listening to this style will help you find interesting phrase ideas so you don't sound stale.

Performance Tips

- Keep notes short and punchy.
- A full warm sound is common in this style.
- The feel should remain strong and pumping.
- This groove should be played on or on top/ahead of the beat.
- Be sure to accent strong beats with the drummer to keep things clear and interesting.
- Vary the eighth note so the strong beats have more weight.
- Try to phrase with the guitar. In this type of song the bass is the low end of the guitar part and should be played mimicking the guitar as closely as possible.

Class Notes: _____

_____

_____

Class Notes: _____

_____

_____

Straight Eighth Boogie Shuffle with Stop Time
CD Track #1 Demo / Track #2 Play-along

Straight Eighth-note Feel with Stop Time

Intro ♩ = 164

Demo Roadmap
Intro, A, B, C

Chart Roadmap
Intro-A-B (3x), C

SUB-STYLE NO. 2:
Medium Rock Stomp

Brief History

This is a staple of many styles of Rock. The ability to play eighth notes and create a pulse is essential to playing Rock bass.

Preparatory Exercises

Playing steady eighths is what this is based on. Practice playing eighth notes with the metronome at different tempos (for example, open strings, scales, arpeggios). Experiment with where you are sitting with the beat (for example, on the beat, in front, or behind). Different tempos lend themselves to different treatment.

Performance Tips

- A fat sound helps fill this out; a little warmth or even a "little" distortion can't hurt.
- On the beat or behind or even a little ahead can work with this. Different parts of the tune can be played with separate feel.
- Try to help balance the time feel between the guitar and drums. Be the glue!
- Don't be afraid to pick an appropriate spot in the breaks between the lick to play a fill now and then; just don't get in the guitarist's or the drummer's way.
- Keep the unison line short and punchy, and lock with the phrasing of the guitar.

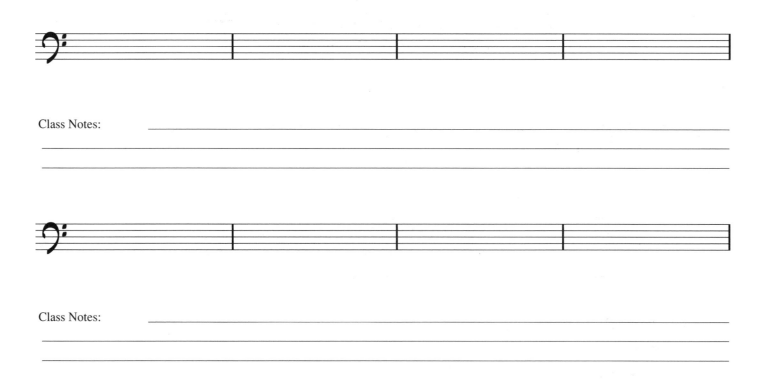

Class Notes: _____

_____

_____

Class Notes: _____

_____

_____

Medium Rock Stomp

Demo Roadmap
Intro, A, B, C

Chart Roadmap
Intro-A-B (4x), C

SUB-STYLE NO. 3:
Rock Ballad

Brief History

The Rock Ballad, or the Power Ballad, is a form that never goes out of style, no matter how it is dressed up, be it heavy or light, ethereal or atomic. This formula goes back to Elvis, Frank Sinatra and others. Many bands have made their careers on one song; don't underestimate the power of a good ballad to reach your audience.

Preparatory Exercises

Ballads demand great tone and long notes, due to the slower tempos. Practice whole notes, half notes, and quarter notes with the metronome at the slowest tempos you can manage, while still keeping the groove. Try to get the maximum note value from each note.

Performance Tips

- Ballads need to be orchestrated. This means planning the use of tone or sound, dynamics, fills, etc in the scheme of the song.
- That being said, fills at the end of phrases can and should be varied to keep things fresh. Predictable is good; boring is not.
- Dynamics are extremely important to help make the song exciting. Know the dynamic road map for the song, i.e., where to build and crescendo and where to pull back.
- Be aware of phrasing. Is it 4 bar, 8 bar, odd or unusual phrasing?

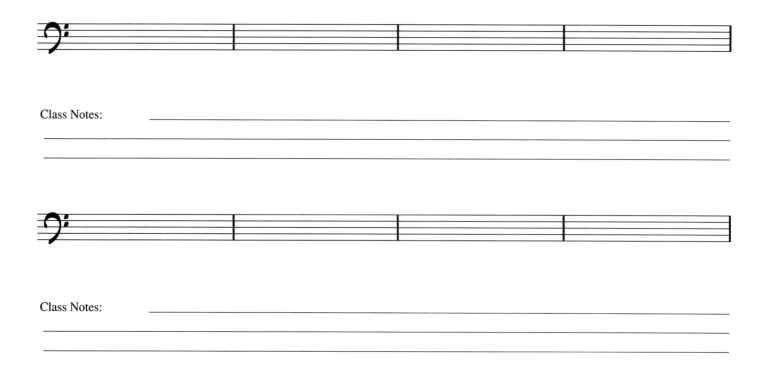

Class Notes: _____

_____

_____

Class Notes: _____

_____

_____

Rock Ballad
CD Track #5 Demo / Track #6 Play-along

Rock Ballad

Demo Roadmap
A, B, C

Chart Roadmap
A-B (3x), C

Class Notes: _____

_____

_____

SUB-STYLE NO. 4:
Funk Rock

Brief History

Funk Rock goes back to the 50s. James Brown is but one of the godfathers of Soul and Rock. Many Rock bassists have based their careers on the work of James Jamerson for Motown. Larry Graham with Sly and the Family Stone established an ideal of the marriage of funk and rock that many have made use of: Miles Davis, Jimi Hendrix, Prince, Parliament Funkadelic, Fishbone, the Red Hot Chili Peppers, and the list continues to grow.

Preparatory Exercises

Practice funk patterns with the metronome for long stretches. Learn to let the time breathe, and not to become boring or mechanical. Machines can never replace us, because their time is too perfect. To be human is to be imperfect.

A strong one or downbeat gives the music an anchor for the time to come back to in a cyclical fashion. Funk is a rhythmic dialogue.

Performance Tips

Funk has many sounds and techniques that can be utilized to give a song a characteristic sound. The sound of a Mutron envelope filter, the effects of phasing or chorus, the use of slapping or tapping, the use of a pick, or palm muting, show that there are no limits to the possibilities: even little mallets taped to your fingers, a la Tony Levin with Peter Gabriel.

Funk is about the groove; the sound is the window dressing that sells the groove. If you are going to hear a lick over and over, it should have an interesting sound.

Class Notes: _____

_____

_____

Class Notes: _____

_____

_____

Funk Rock
CD Track #7 Demo/ Track #8 Play-along

Funk Rock

Demo Roadmap
A, B, C

Chart Roadmap
A-B (3x), C

SUB-STYLE NO. 5:
Heavy Rock

Brief History

Heavy Rock has existed since the 60s and has been popularized by groups like Led Zeppelin, AC DC, Black Sabbath and countless others since. Characterized by powerful riffs and mountain-moving volume, it's the music that generated a sea of tiny fists, not to mention lighters.

Preparatory Exercises

The triplet section of this song exhibits how triplets can change up a groove and provide a new and fresh section to a song. Practice playing half-note, quarter-note, eighth-note, and sixteenth-note triplets against a quarter-note click. The ability to go back and forth from 4 to 3 (and 3 to 4) opens up a wealth of rhythmic vocabulary.

Performance Tips

Powerful grooves need a strong foundation. To quote Gene Simmons of KISS, "Rock-guitar power chords don't exist without the bass playing a low note underneath." Building the wall of powerful sound that defines much of heavy rock takes an understanding of pacing and dynamics as well as an ability to provide a low-end sonic backdrop that the grand drama of the music is played out against.

The open Es in the A-section can be made more interesting by adding sixteenth accents. Practice substituting combinations of sixteenths for the eighths until you find combinations that lock with the guitar and drums and are more interesting than the straight eighths.

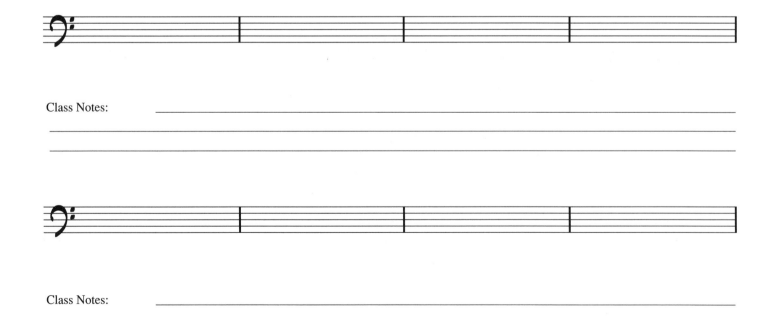

Class Notes: _____

_____

_____

Class Notes: _____

_____

_____

Heavy Rock

Demo Roadmap
A1, A2, B1, B2 (first 4 bars of each)

Chart Roadmap
A1–A2–B1–B2 (2x)

SUB-STYLE NO. 6:
Traditional Shuffle

Brief History

The traditional shuffle is just one of the Blues' many contributions to Rock. It's often hard to tell where one leaves off and the other begins. Rock's blues roots are easy to trace, from Chuck Berry to Clapton to Stevie Ray Vaughn, not to mention Led Zeppelin and the Rolling Stones. An ability to walk a blues and groove on a shuffle should be a part of every rock bassist's repertoire.

Preparatory Exercises

Play the blues form at various tempos with the metronome, from very slow to very fast. Be able to get a smooth groove that rocks at any tempo and be able to hold it for as long as the solos might go on; in some bands that could be a while. It takes practice and concentration, but the power of a good shuffle to grab an audience is hard to deny.

Performance Tips

Getting a good tone that complements the instrumentation you're performing with is the key. Rock-guitar sounds can be quite different in tone and texture. How we as bassists choose to complement them gives Rock an even broader sense of variety. Even simple patterns, playing the root, or arpeggios for instance, if played at different parts of the fingerboard take on a different color, tone, edge, warmth, etc. Moving patterns around to different octaves gives the music motion without disturbing continuity. No one wants to bore their audience; music needs to constantly evolve but still be cohesive in some fashion for the audience to be able to relate to it.

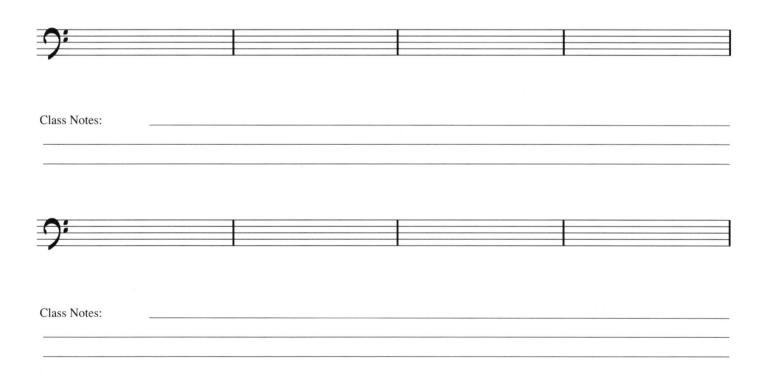

Class Notes: _____

_____

_____

Class Notes: _____

_____

_____

Traditional Shuffle

Demo Roadmap
Intro, A, C

Chart Roadmap
Intro, A-B (2x), C

SUB-STYLE NO. 7:
Hard Rock Shuffle

Brief History

The Hard Rock Shuffle was popularized by many British bands ranging from Queen to Zeppelin, the list is endless. Texas boys such as ZZ Top and Stevie Ray Vaughan have kept it alive. The Hard Rock Shuffle incorporates all the hallmarks of the traditional shuffle with a little more power and drive.

Preparatory Exercises

Practice the shuffle groove with the metronome using the changes from the lead sheet.

Performance Tips

- The feel should be loose and flowing, contrasted by the accents at the end of phrases that break the flow and capture the audience's attention.
- Be generous with the hits in the intro. The two falloffs can be exaggerated for character. It can be very tight or very sloppy depending on the desired effect.
- In the bars 1, 2, 5 and 6 of the B-section, be sure to slide from the Root (D) up to the third (F♯).
- Fingering should be first finger on D (A-string, 5th Fret) sliding with 3 or 4 to the F♯ (A- string, 9th fret). This puts the A (D-string, 7th fret) under the first finger and the B (D-string, 9th fret) under the 3rd or 4th finger.

Class Notes: _____
_____
_____

Class Notes: _____
_____
_____

Class Notes: _____
_____
_____

Hard Rock Shuffle
CD Track #13 Demo / Track #14 Play-along

Hard Rock Shuffle

Demo Roadmap
Intro A, B, C

Chart Roadmap
Intro, A-B (2x), C

SUB-STYLE NO. 8:
$\frac{12}{8}$ Slow Blues [minor]

Brief History

Another contribution from the world of blues, the $\frac{12}{8}$ feel is common in gospel and soul music as well. It's been used in many Rock blues classics from Hendrix and Zeppelin to the Rolling Stones.

Preparatory Exercises

The underpinning of three in this piece gives it a lilt, a sway, that without which it becomes just slow and, in a worst-case scenario, tedious. It is important to be able to bring out this swing in the music. Playing the blues form at a really slow tempo is an art; using the $\frac{12}{8}$ or triplet feel makes the slowest tempos have a groove. Play with the metronome as slowly as you can. Play the $\frac{12}{8}$ blues feel until you feel confident that you are creating a groove that swings.

Performance Tips

- A big sound is helpful to fill up the space in a slow-moving tune without playing a lot of notes. Make sure to hold notes for their fullest values.
- Connecting the notes creates a cushion of sound.
- The fills at the end of bars are all triplets. They lock into the $\frac{12}{8}$ feel where the beginning of the phrase is more over the 12, smoothing out some of the motion from the drums and providing homogenous cohesion.

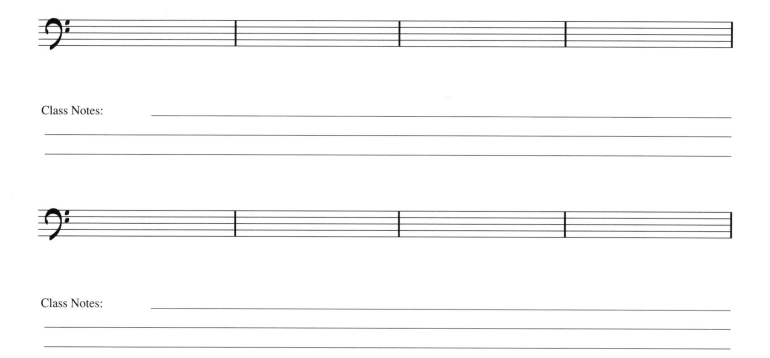

Class Notes: _____

_____

_____

Class Notes: _____

_____

_____

⏺ ¹²⁄₈ Slow Blues (minor)
CD Track #15 Demo / Track #16 Play-along

¹²⁄₈ Slow Blues (minor)

Demo Roadmap
Intro, A (take the 2nd ending only)

Chart Roadmap
Intro, A (take the 1st and 2nd endings)

SUB-STYLE NO. 9:
2-Beat

Brief History

A staple of Jazz, Country, and Rockabilly, not to mention the tuba in New Orleans music, the bass playing with a 2-feel never goes out of style. It adds contrast and leaves space that can open up a song or section. This particular example has a New Orleans pop flavor that comes from songs in the late 1950s and early 60s.

Preparatory Exercises

1. Experiment with the different tones you can derive from the bass by changing your right-hand position. Examine all the possibilities from over the end of the neck for a warm natural, acoustic sound, to back by the bridge for a bright, tight, punchy sound.

2. Find a spot near the neck where you can comfortably play and get an acoustic-bass sound. A versatile bassist has many spots where the right hand gets a different sound. Every bassist should have a minimum of two areas where they are comfortable: one for warm and natural sound and one closer to the bridge for a more contemporary sound.

3. Being an interesting bassist involves having different facets to your style. The ability to tailor your sound to the style of music you're playing at any given moment is invaluable in making music that is unique and interesting.

Performance Tips

- This particular style developed when either the tuba or acoustic bass supplied the bass function. Mimicking the tone and phrasing of these instruments provides authenticity to classic grooves.
- Plucking or picking the bass closer to the neck rather than near the bridge will help warm and fatten your tone naturally.
- The classic 2-feel is much harder than it seems.
- The music needs to swing just as hard with the bass playing half as much.
- The bass playing on beats 1 and 3 is answered/balanced by the snare drum on 2 and 4. This sets up a musical seesaw that propels the music forward.
- The tension and release generated creates a powerful driving feel.

Class Notes: _____

_____

_____

2-Beat

Play 4 times

Demo Roadmap
A, B, C

Chart Roadmap
A-B (4x), C

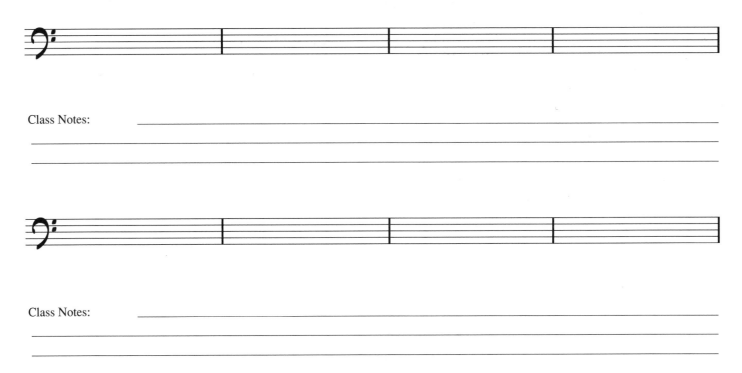

Class Notes: _____

Class Notes: _____

SUB-STYLE NO. 10:
Train Beat (Country Shuffle)

Brief History

Another contribution from the Country and Rockabilly side of Rock, this is a wide-open groove that has lots of potential to move people. Most of what was said about the 2-feel holds true for the Train Beat, sometimes called the Country Shuffle. This is an even more straight and classic approach to feeling the music in 2.

Today's Country music has much in common with Rock and Pop. Many of these "feels" have a home in Country, Rock, Rockabilly, Bluegrass, Country Swing, and Pop.

Preparatory Exercises

Play in 2 using the changes from this song or a blues. Use the metronome and try having it click only on beats 2 and 4 while you are playing on 1and 3. Try this at different tempos to master the art of 2 in any situation.

Performance Tips

- This is another style that owes much to the acoustic bass and tuba.
- Using the most natural acoustic sound is the tradition in this style.
- Review the Performance Tips for the 2-Beat (Sub-Style No. 9) as they apply equally in this style.

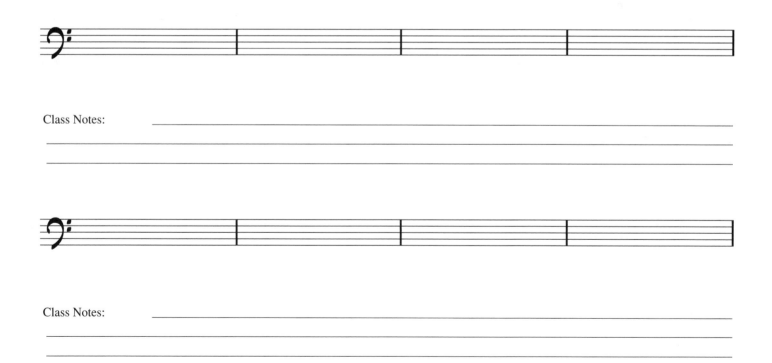

Class Notes: _____

_____

_____

Class Notes: _____

_____

_____

Train Beat (Country Shuffle)
CD Track #19 Demo / Track #20 Play-along

Train Beat (Country Shuffle)

Demo Roadmap
A, B, C

Chart Roadmap
A-B (4x), C

SUB-STYLE NO. 11:
"Bo Diddley" Beat

Brief History

Derived from the New Orleans groove based on the clave pattern from Latin music, this beat has been part of Rock since its very beginning. From the Rolling Stones to modern Rap/Hip-Hop, this groove, with roots in Africa, is a surefire way to fill up a dance floor.

The B-section takes the feel to a more contemporary rock feel, reminiscent of Little Feat or the Meters/Neville Brothers.

Preparatory Exercises

Take the first two bars of the chart and play the figure for a few minutes with the metronome. Start at a slow tempo and then advance to faster one in medium increments.

Performance Tips

Be aware of the differences between the two sections of the song. The two grooves are very similar but should be distinct from each other so that the song's two sections are contrasted.

Class Notes: _____

_____

_____

Class Notes: _____

_____

_____

Class Notes: _____

_____

_____

"Bo Diddley" Beat
CD Track #21 / Track #22 Play-along

Note: There are two common ways to notate the "Bo Diddley" Beat: 1) with the clave groove in one bar or 2) over two bars as notated here.

"Bo Diddley" Beat

Demo Roadmap
A, B, A (6 measures), Coda

Chart Roadmap
A-B (3x), A (6 measures), Coda

SUB-STYLE NO. 12:
New Orleans Second Line

Brief History

This style is epitomized by New Orleans groups like The Meters, Neville Bros., Dr. John, Little Feat, The Wild Tchoupitoulas, and Gatemouth Brown. New Orleans is a city to which Rock owes a great debt. Much of what we know as Rock has roots in the Jazz, Blues, and parade music of the Crescent City.

Preparatory Exercises

Try to expand on the feel developed with the "Bo Diddley" beat. This groove has a high potential for funk that will keep dancers of all ages grooving. Find the deep pocket in this style, and your band mates and audience will thank you.

Performance Tips

- This style demands a loose relaxed feel.
- Slurs and slides only add to the second-line funk of this groove.
- The feel between the instruments should never get tense. This is good-time party music. *Laisez le bon temps roulet!*

Class Notes: _____

_____

_____

Class Notes: _____

_____

_____

New Orleans Second Line
CD Track #23 Demo / Track #24 Play-along

New Orleans Second Line

Demo Roadmap
A, B, C

Chart Roadmap
A-B (3x), C

SUB-STYLE NO. 13:
Up-tempo Rock-Swing with Stop Time (Rockabilly)

Brief History

This style is directly descended from Jazz, Blues, Boogie-woogie and Jump Swing. From the 1930s onward, this driving rhythm has thrilled audiences across generations. At faster tempos it has the effect of a freight train coming down the tracks. Generating powerful forward motion, this style has inspired dancers to fashionable excess.

Preparatory Exercises

Practice arpeggios and simple repetitive walking patterns at all tempos. The goal is to be able to keep up the energy and driving feel at fast tempos, while keeping the feel relaxed, but never frantic. Technical proficiency needs to be above what you think you will need. If you think you'll play a song like this for five minutes, you should be able to practice playing it for ten minutes nonstop, and feel comfortable and relaxed, and ready to continue. That way, in five minutes you will never get tired or run out of ideas.

Performance Tips

This style swings but in a straighter sense than most Jazz. It is not a shuffle feel. Arpeggios, walking lines and melodic patterns are all good sources of harmonic material.

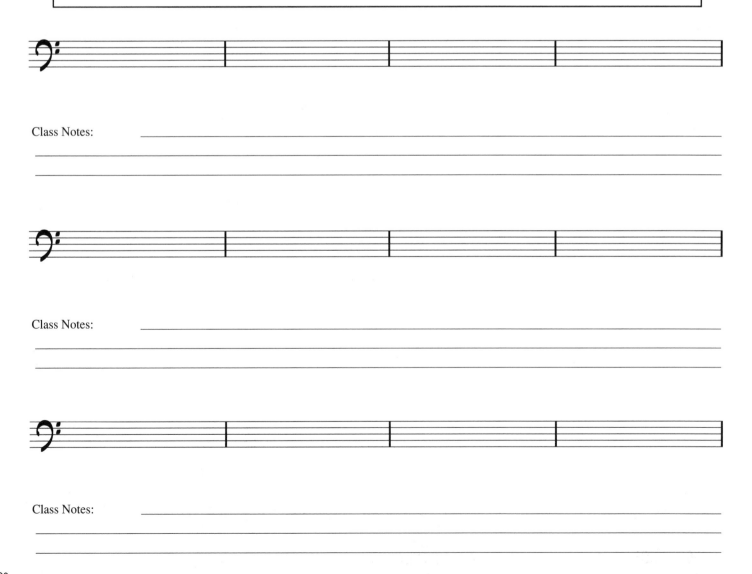

Class Notes: _____

_____

_____

Class Notes: _____

_____

_____

Class Notes: _____

_____

_____

Up-tempo Rock-Swing with Stop Time
CD Track #25 Demo / Track #26 Play-along

Up-tempo Rock-Swing with Stop Time

♩ = 240

A E7

B C♯

E7 C♯

E7

A7 C♯ Play 3 times

C E7

A7 C♯7

E7

Demo Roadmap
A, B, C

Chart Roadmap
A-B (3x), C

SUB-STYLE NO. 14:
Reggae

Brief History

Reggae and Rock have borrowed from each other a great deal over the years. Artists like Bob Marley certainly had knowledge of Rock. Artists like The Police are Rock musicians who have learned and utilized the language of Reggae. This is evocative of the two-way street of influence that Rock exhibits with many other styles. It's what keeps Rock alive; a constant influx of new ideas from whatever music a culture has to offer.

Preparatory Exercises

The best preparation one can have for Reggae is to have listened to it as played by the masters. Aston "Family Man" Barrett with Bob Marley and others and Robbie Shakespeare from the Rhythm duo Sly and Robbie are excellent bassists and exemplify some of the best Reggae bass the music has to offer. Sting's early work with the Police shows how the tradition can be adapted to Rock and Pop sensibilities.

Performance Tips

- The hardest aspect of some styles is the absence of a key element we are accustomed to relying on, in this case "the one." Rock, like most of Western music, relies on the one, the first beat, the starting point. Reggae frequently upsets the normal approach by leaving out the one.
- Reggae bass makes great use of space. Sparse and catlike one moment, busy and melodic the next, always in the pocket, it can start at any point in the bar. The "and" of one, two, and of two, three, four, there's a Reggae feel that can start anywhere.
- Once the pattern begins, it rarely stops. The hypnotic trance-like quality transports everyone present to a primitive ritual where time stands still as the music unfolds.
- Play the 2nd bar of the A-section, (the answer) with the Cs alternating with open As (C-A-C-A sixteenth notes). The open strings add bounce to the line.

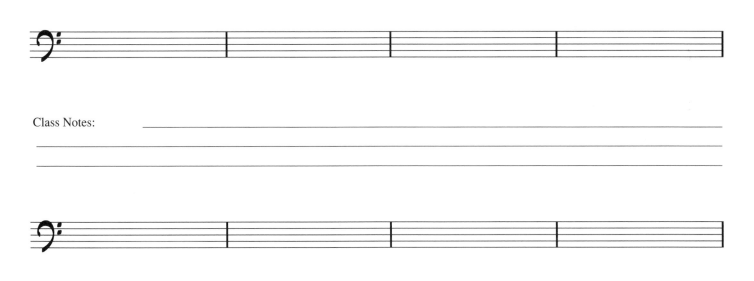

Class Notes: _____

_____

_____

Class Notes: _____

_____

_____

Reggae

A ♩ = 130
Dm

B Gm   C7

Gm   C7   Gm   C7   Gm   C7

Play 2 times

Am   D7   Am   D7   Am   D7   Em   D7

Demo Roadmap
A, B

Chart Roadmap
A-B (2x)

Class Notes: _____

SUB-STYLE NO. 15:
Rockin' Odd Meters

Brief History

Odd meters started appearing in Rock in the 1960s but really started to be more prominent since the 70s. The earliest instances came from classically trained musicians playing Rock. This group of musicians led the vanguard of what was the birth of so-called progressive rock, groups like King Crimson, Yes, Emerson Lake and Palmer, Pink Floyd, Led Zeppelin, Frank Zappa, and John McLaughlin's Mahavishnu Orchestra, all laid the groundwork for what many musicians since have taken for granted: namely, that any type of rhythm can be adapted to a Rock format. This continues today with many of the heaviest and hardest Rock bands using odd meters.

Preparatory Exercises

Using the metronome, practice each section of the piece separately. The three different time feels must be mastered individually before you can put them together. Try them at a slow tempo until you feel the time. We don't count $\frac{4}{4}$; we feel it. Odd meters should be approached the same way. Once you can feel the natural flow of the music it becomes easy to hear phrases and not be stuck playing an ostinato pattern.

Performance Tips

- Becoming comfortable with the individual time feels is the starting point. This will allow you to anticipate metric shifts comfortably and make smoother transitions between them.
- The A-section could be played down an octave if you have a five- or six-string bass. Alternating A-sections you could play it as written the first time and the second time down an octave, giving the song an arrangement idea and a small change that gives the second A-section more depth because it is an octave lower.
- Subtle shifts can help shape a song's pacing and dynamics, keeping listeners interested without using large changes that may upset the delicate balance odd meters sometimes present.

Class Notes: _____

_____

_____

Class Notes: _____

_____

_____

Rockin' Odd Meters
CD Track #29 Demo / Track #30 Play-along

Rockin' Odd Meters

Demo Roadmap
A (8 measures), B, C (2x)

Chart Roadmap
A-B (3x), C (4x)

Selected Bibliography

Kaye, Carol. *Bass Method*. www.carolkaye.com.

Motown Bass Classics, transcribed by Steve Gorenberg. Hal Leonard Corporation.

Rock Bass Bible. Hal Leonard Corporation.

Slutsky, Allan "Dr. Licks." *Standing in the Shadows of Motown: The Life and Music of Legendary Bassist James Jamerson*. Hal Leonard Publishing Corporation.

Slutsky, Allan "Dr. Licks" and Silverman, Chuck. *The Funkmasters. The James Brown Rhythm Sections: 1960–1973*. Manhattan Music, Inc. a Warner Bros. Publication Company (1977).

Tindall, Tim. *What Duck Done: That's Soul Folks*! Stax Record Co./Fantasy Inc. (1994).

Selected Discography

Elvis Presley: The Complete Sun Sessions

Rolling Stones (Greatest Hits)

The Beatles (Greatest Hits)

Motown Singles Collection

Elton John (Greatest Hits)

Best of Booker T. and the MG's

Best of the Meters

Steely Dan: Aja, Gaucho, Pretzel Logic

Led Zeppelin Complete Recordings

Black Sabbath Paranoid

Free (Greatest Hits)

Red Hot Chili Peppers (Greatest Hits)

The Police (Greatest Hits)

Bob Marley (Greatest Hits)

Queen (Greatest Hits)

Rush (Greatest Hits)

Bo Diddley (Greatest Hits)

Cream (Greatest Hits)

Best of Eric Clapton

Primus: Sailing the Sea of Cheese

Tower of Power (Greatest Hits)

The Who: Live at Leeds

Best of the Beach Boys

collective
Contemporary Styles Series

BOOKS WITH CDs

The material in The Collective Contemporary Styles Series represents many years of work on the part of many talented Collective faculty members, who have the experience of playing and teaching these styles to literally thousands of young rhythm-section musicians over the last thirty years. This series is the fruit of their labor and talent with the information presented in a manner that is easy to grasp.

CO1 **Afro-Caribean & Brazilian Rhythms for the Drums**
By Memo Acevedo, Frank Katz, Chris Lacinak, Kim Plainfield, Adrian Santos, and Maciek Schijbal

CO2 **Afro-Caribean & Brazilian Rhythms for the Bass**
By Lincoln Goines, Steve Marks, Nilson Matta, Irio O'Farill and Leo Traversa

CO3 **Fusion: A Study in Contemporary Music for the Drums**
By Kim Plainfield

CO4 **Fusion: A Study in Contemporary Music for the Bass**
By Leo Traversa

CO5 **Contemporary Rock Styles for the Drums**
By Sandy Gennaro

CO6 **Contemporary Rock Styles for the Bass**
By Gary Kelly

CO7 **Contemporary Jazz Styles for the Drums**
By Ian Froman and Peter Retzlaff

CO8 **Contemporary Jazz Styles for the Bass**
By Joe Fitzgerald and Hilliard Greene

CO9 **Contemporary R&B and Funk Styles for the Drums**
By Pat Petrillo

CO10 **Contemporary R&B and Funk Styles for the Bass**
By Frank Gravis and Steve Marks

CO11 **Contemporary Hip Hop and Drum 'n' Bass Styles for the Drums**
By Guy Licata

CO12 **Contemporary Hip Hop and Drum 'n' Bass Styles for the Bass**
By John Davis

CARL FISCHER
MUSIC